Santa Fe... the swagger of the ransom of the made-up
funeral   "Leave me alone Tony Randall" All accidents are
intentional, but they're still accidents, buddy... "The planets
that are our brains orbit fitfully" Look at Richard playing
the piano with that shitface grin... I've gotta go steal some
whiskey now to drink with Ol' Roison the Beau... Take a look
at a teenage harmony... "I got angry at the wastebasket
there..." Some poets have images passing through their
eyes like melting ore until their sockets seal shut ... Shafer,
hand, foot, etc ... "his lungs are well supplied with blood"
"Lemme get one of them Roman Coin datebooks"   With
rocks, salt and nails... We don't have to take this one down
Garth... "To own a boat must be a pleasure"

— **Eddie Berrigan**

Never Cry Woof

Never Cry Woof

Shafer Hall

Illustrations by
Amanda Burnham

No Tell Books 2007
Reston, VA

for Mom, Grace,

Dad, and Richard

Contents

2.

How to Survive on Land & Sea

Evening came
with no nickels for dancing.

Earlier in the day,
a public opinion poll
of two Mexican kids indicated:
one hundred percent
of two Mexican kids
prefer orange Popsicles
to their big brother's girl.

From which it can be inferred
that life is like a train
and we are like cheap apartments
and we shake when the train rolls by.

See for yourself:
in the nickel light
a slender woman dances
and mispronounces your name.

Dental Gold

A few folks back home got blue-chip mouths;
once Pepper Stevens told me
his grill could attract catfish
when he smiled at night by the river.

Elegance standing
in walls of teeth
incisors – a sunrise.

Nick Burnette's America

"Roy Orbison's sublime,"
say Nick's four-year old eyes.

Nick provides
incisive commentary

(suburban decay,
middle-age paranoia)

by throwing a brick through
my uncle's rotted back fence.

"Nick," I say, watching him eat,
"I had forgotten the beauty of *banana*."

Evelyn's Kitchen

The sun from the late afternoon
staples the tiles to the counter
in Evelyn's kitchen. It staples me
to this moment in her chair.

Evelyn emerges apron-tied
from the back of her house;
she can move freely despite the chilly light.

She moves around with tasks I cannot premonish
until they are performed. They involve
vegetables and blades and other devices.

What roiling ritual is this?
What does this dance mean?
Where are the shapes that I know?

Brian Orsak's Tuxedo

Laying around on him
like a curse:
these threads
as well-tailored
as his anger
at the incursion
of this cocktail party.

He stands,
the very invention
of clay modeling, still;
his lungs are well supplied with blood.

Frances's Fine Lines

This form,
now failed
to function,

founded
in profound beauty,
if not
forged in Detroit,

lies,
funereal,
in the family home,
while those of us
who feared her in life
take a free ride.

(I dare you to kiss her!)

Important Information About Your Man

cold trucks and curves
the South risen for the
seconds counted that make
the body of Fall

whining evening, winding
through easy nouns
like "eats" and "stop"

to hide the smells she made
he removed his skin

Demon Rub

To the self-destructive comfort
of the sound of the TV at night
and back, he dragged himself
like a truck.

With a pair of looks
petrified in his eyes,
he blamed and flirted
with himself in the mirror.

And you should thank
your lucky stars
you weren't around
to see it.

Nannies Love Their Own Children Too

the no-sound of pitch dripping from pine
the end of sound

ends
met praise

a brittle siege
a turning of leaves

the no-sound of varnish hardening on pine
the end of sound

and, at the end of the hitch
the beginning of night

Pink Snow

Resolution for any time of year:
to respect the animals out in the yard,
and let them crawl about in peace
for awhile, for they are smaller creatures,
even the bulls are smaller than me.

Gentry landed me in this mess
of haystacks and merciful slaughter;
I am gentle with my ax – and quick;
I am sure of my hand;
it will occasionally slip.

Warm ground soaks right up,
but snow remembers awhile.

Avery's Possums

The horror;
a five-year-old girl's
intransitive loathing
finds an object
in a blissfully ignorant
marsupial.

Let spring blossom,
little possum, your world
is worse than you know.
Keep your rat's teeth clean
on the pinewood of my fence;
let the shadow you cast
on my bedroom wall be large.

Sunflowers are monsters
to the mice in the field.

Terror

Count the Ts on your tongue:
Forget. Tuxedo. Azteca.

Now knit several Ss into
a blanket for your mouth:
Estoy. Some sort of providence.

Give yourself some room, now,
with silent sounds:
Knot. Knowingly.

Now pronounce the commas
As, you, try, to, get, away.

John Gotti is Haunting Jamison from Beyond the Grave

Why the sleepless nights, Jamison?

Are you aghast
at the indignity
of all those rampant mourners
eating tragedy?

Or would some maligned authority
have you stone-tablet everybody,
telling us of the beauty that will be
when we all hang on ropes from trees?

And what of your woman
as her arm is ripped from its socket
when you wake up, sweating, in the night?

John Gotti: His fury is gravity.
The planets that are our brains
orbit fitfully.

Akron, Cold Beer, and Poor, Poor Thing

The Doctor is in; Mike Mahoney is in.
He started at the edge of light,
and now his office is a bit like a Midwestern jail,
both hot and cold at the same time.

Fiddling with the door, he confirms its status: locked
like a late-evening Super Bowl bet. The doctor is in.

On the end of the beach, fiddling with childhood memories,
Dr. Mike Mahoney finally remembers where,
on a hot night on Aransas Pass in 1977, he left himself

in a sense.

A Sunday Brunch Ordeal

The refined use of cutlery's rules
suspended like a mobile midair,
Aunt Cindy will do the talking for
your lungs, they're hard as coconuts.

Click, click: It's actually a drip
that your mind is misinterpreting
in its paralysis; you clench your teeth
and tell yourself: I want to be that sincere.

Mornings like these are a longing
for no curtains, for rats
unimpeded by traps, for irons, for quiet,
for a cold home made of stone.

Holiday in Mt. Kisco

After one thousand years on trial, Robert Phelps returned
     home to Mount Kisco;
he decided to take a few days off before he returned to
     work.

He spent the first few hours taking a nap, and then he took
     a long shower and ate
a large meal of trout and blackberries that his wife cooked
     using a recipe that she
had channeled from Outer Space.

He finished off the evening throwing the baseball with his
     son.

His time was spent just the way you would imagine a man
     would spend it,
who had just come home after a long absence, minus any
     sort of relations
between himself and his wife.

Libido, it seems, suspended itself, for Bob Phelps' return to
     Mt. Kisco.

And Then The Whole Place Got Light

After that, things
started happening on their own.

The lawsuit brought itself
against the police department,

money silently left
the bank accounts of the insurance company,

different money quietly
replaced it;

the man and his wounds buried
themselves, by the book, in the ground,

while the clouds grayed themselves
and dutifully entered the scene.

His eulogy wrote itself, it seemed,
while my desk chair spun slowly and thoughtfully
in front of my desk.

Near Magical Skills

Near to God
he lived, he said,
he claimed
he was close
to God.

Fat, waddling
his swagger was a swagger
of the soul and not the body,
the ransom note of history
was never slipped into his pocket.

Laying like a house
on the table, dead
as a pile of rocks
as he always
thought he should be,
nearly magical,
smiling,
me crying,

he filled his suit
like a fucking man.

Upon the Death of a Fish

Weep for me,
You friends who
Still can weep,

Herman, the
Little carp,
Is belly-up!

It's Christmas
Time and my soul
Is very small,

I had some
Gin to make
Me tall again.

Herman's eyes
Begged for that
Medicine - who

Among us
Could deny a
Fish a drink?

And my mistress,
She will have
My skin.

Cathy

Folks these days talk a lot
about where Rock & Roll's gone off to lately
leaving us all so lonely and high

I don't think I'll tell them
that I kissed it over the Charles
where the Mass Ave. bridge starts to rise

T-Bone & T-Bone's Old Lady

The weather is cold in Houston now,
one of the few cold days of the year.

Some of us walk around in t-shirts anyway,
those of us without wives, I guess.

T-Bone's old lady gave me some of her onion,
but it didn't help my stomach.

T-Bone just laughs and laughs
about everything at all.

Shaw on Dickens

I placed Tale of Two Cities on top of Arms and the Man,
and in between them I placed a couple fingernails.

In a short while, I started to think that maybe Tale of Two
was too much weight for my fingernails,
and, irrationally, the ends of my fingers felt uncomfortable.

So, I removed Arms from Tale,
placed Tale on the floor,
gently lay my fingernails on top of Tale,
and placed Arms on top.

The Last Days of Blue Cotton Jerseys Schooled Catfish in the Art of Long Blonde Golden Hair

it was the yellow bus ride, it was
a yellow moon of golden hair
winking at me over a green seat

I lived for a little slaw, maybe
or maybe for a warm yellow jacket

I needed a small yellow sound, high,
girlish

"Hnnn"

Catfish left
a feminine hygiene product
in my jeans

Turtle Wax

Epsom salt and the beginning of time,
fire ants storming up the hill like marines,
and I had a red bicycle that I named "Rambo."

The contraptions on the playground, then,
were big as brontosauruses,
and they burned in the sunlight.

I heard that oleander leaves were poisonous,
so I ate a handful.

"If you don't get inside they'll be carbon-
dating samples of you eons from now!"
mothers yell, out into the darkening eve.

Years later, waxing my car,
I chew an oleander leaf;
my car is named Honda.

Crossworld

glazeddoughnuts is how I compare
the seamless run-on or more likely
car-chase of life's arc from youth

pigeontoed
to maturity
across the sea
Edoed Tokyoed

gazing east to the west
surrounding bare-chest
friends pound up jamesjoyce
pillows like breasts

noise, and I will
make a mental note:

the chair was ombudsmeant
to make the most of the rope

Winter Coney

Off the train
And down the ramp
And we are the third
And fourth men
On the moon

The Rent In My Mouth

Jawing,
jaw dropping,
we watched the teeth falling
and shuddered at the sound they made
when they landed on the marble floor.

It's expensive in here.

Central Patricia

In the great ice mines
of southern Canada,
they make water
by melting ore in their
red hot mouths.

The gold flows
less preciously there;
their teeth all are
made of metal
cooled in snow.

Patricia explores
herself, most of her
is made of water
in the form of lakes
and melted glaciers.

Falling In Love With New Jersey

Getting away with something
underneath the Hudson River,
through the Lincoln Tunnel,
into the broad, wooded cosmos
on the mainland,

he walked like a person:
not hiding behind pickup trucks,
not turning his collar up against his ears,

through
parking lot, field, parking lot,
field, house, house, supermarket,

experiencing an experiment
in civil engineering.

Apple Parts: A Pre-Packaged Berkshire Odyssey

Holding a broomstick over your head:
concentrate on your brother's hand
and on the green apple he is holding.

Let the sun turn green, brown, red and yellow
trees all to white, ground to white,
brother's red sweater to white;
the green apple will rip across it all
like green on white.

When you swing the broom, concentrate
on the things you said last night
that humiliate you now.

Exploding crabapple: your salvation.

Every Three Hundred Nights

Let us make a trade:

a topographical map of my body
for a bas-relief of your mind;

these items will have to do,
in a pinch or for a thousand years.

Every three hundred nights,
we will restore our rights
to one another's favorite parts.

When I lay on the grass in the park,
I shall break no blades.

The Evening Wore Blue

Last night, we went prowling down Second Avenue,
and I wore my favorite shirt,
hoping with aim but without conviction
that Anna would be back from L.A.
and once again patrolling the Lower East Side.

I stunned myself
when I walked around a corner
and saw the evening;
it had out-dressed me
in blues and stars.

"Aha, Anna," I thought,
"West."

A Love Poem (Me-oh My-oh)

The sexy (sultry,
pipe-swinging) sound
of a 1972 Chevelle.

Sometimes,
in front of the mirror
dressed in bluejeans
and a white undershirt,
I can almost convince myself:
I am Tom Jones!

Thrumm, chugga chugga chugga.

Conspiratory Poem Addressing All Imaginable Possibilities

Two people in different boroughs could not survive
putting their heads together at one time;
such plans require feet and chests and hips;
these also have to get together or get near,
so everything ends up an ardent mess on an evening pier.

Arms can move a head, that's the trouble;
feet argue constantly with other feet
and treat the ground poorly.
Pretty soon it's Friday night,
and there are a bunch of people together making people.

Oh, horrible conspiracies! Oh summer sun groping down
into New Jersey! Spare us the periods and the condoms,
the commas and prosthetics; those two people necking
in the park are committing luxurious crime after crime!
She is a wheelbarrow; he is a wheelchair.

Ah, a little paranoia is a comfortable thing;
a lot of that sex is only what people do with their pets,
and on the return of steady breath sensuality is no longer
a bad witch in a pleather-sticky dress.

So I walked freely around with the slanted clouds
floating uptown; my lightning was unzipped,
but on my way to meet you I realized that there was fog
all over my notion, so I perspired
into Daybreak: Northern Hemis-Fire.

The Evolution of Miriam Barbary

You're Barbary to me.
Be my Barbary.
Barbary is the end and the Beginningbary.
Your name is a call to Barbary.
Barbary as catch can.

Watching Polish girls Xerox their faces and asses,
trying to make heads or tails of evolution.
Barbary, Barbary, Barbary.

Fighting bold colors for fighting;
the story of Polish evolution.
Miriam, Miriam, Miriam
Barbary.

Something Blue

Late at night
With Tony Randall
And something blue.

On the corner of a bed
With Tony Randall
In his hotel room.

Falling out
Of Tony Randall's eyes,
"I'll meet you on the floor

if it doesn't soak me up,
and we can have a Tony Randall party
and invite all the fellas!"

Rapture as
Tony Randall sings
Petals for our ears.

Leave me alone
Tony Randall
Your pleasure is too sublime.

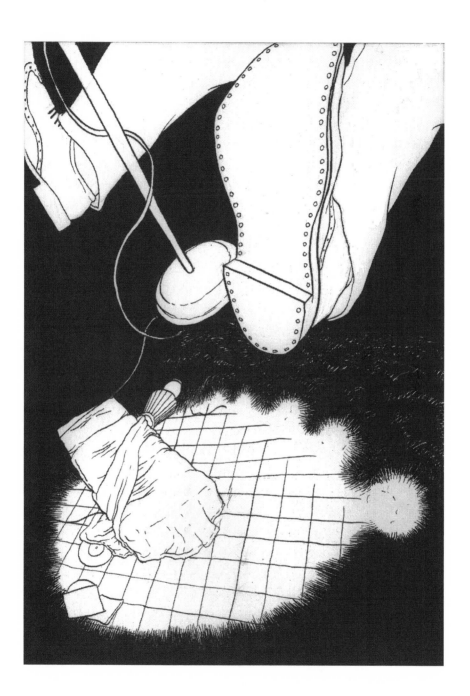

3 Minutes

-Ben Murphy

It takes three
minutes to
cook, but what
shall I do
for the rest
of my life?

Sparking Rail/Trailing Twine

train, train, naked eye,

sparks from the third rail
arc by

then
POLICE ACTION

and the sirens
attenuate through the
tunnels

like coffee cans
and twine

that Amanda's briefcase
will be late to work

is no concern
of mine

Sibilants

in and of themselves, prepositional
like the air-brakes on a train;
they say out loud, "you stop here."

Or occasionally said to themselves,
as when you are trying to sleep or
are sleeping and hiss at sheep,
with everything so quiet
you can hear yourself breathe.

Or all alone in the world:
some ducks flying south.

A Malfunction at the Junction

I found myself bored this morning
on the Marcy Avenue platform,
and, thinking of my old friend Grehlls,
I got angry at the wastebasket there,
called it "Mister!"
and repeatedly asked it
what it was looking at.

Guilt finally bested me.
You're not supposed to talk to trashcans.

I turned my face in shame
until I faced a young Hasidic girl
all locked up in wool

and loosed into the world
a tremendous wink.

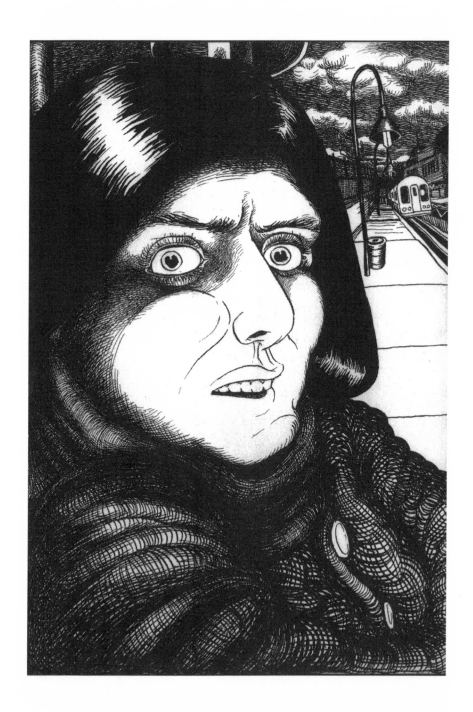

Bare As A Song

A child pulls shingles off a roof
and throws them into the street; the sound,

clap,

of the shingles colliding with the road
will awaken a woman.

And as she walks down the street,
she will love the sound
of her cough against the cold.

And in time, out there, in the liminal,
the object will revolt;
the subject will act upon itself;
the word will make a sound:

Cough!

Some Commotion out My Door at Night

Some commotion,
and the blown-glass end of two tomcats
winked in red blood and hair.

I spent the remainder of the evening
handicapping the marriage of the couple next door

and the next morning
placed a long-term, sure-fire, big-money bet
with the sucker who lives downstairs.

When Black Eyes Go Red

The truth is, they
were yelling to keep
their lungs warm.

I will take up smoking
only for the winter.

Brooklyn Aubade

The king of the animal kingdom,
tongue pressed against his teeth,
released the low whistle that signaled
the beginning of the day.
                              Dawn
and water meet for the aloof
and curious alike; egg creams
and jellybeans are sustenance
too.
        Armed with the thick skin
that covers the knuckles, and
armored with the hubris that
hardens in the fingernails,
the milk that dribbled
down his chin made him
paradoxically more of a man.

Memorial Day

To hold wonder in hand,
starfished and scalloped,
for one perfect minute.

To add another turret
to the castle, just
to add.

To be satisfied:
summer vacation is
the end of the world.

You're Going the Wrong Way, Baby

West is for the birds, baby.

When the smell of afternoon
is getting everybody high,
and all the plants have twisted
their faces in your direction,

I'll keep your name safe, baby,
I'll keep it on the high ridge
of my left shoulder blade.

From the Butcher to His Milkmaid

Cutting fish:
woman, shut your eyes!

The smell of dairy on a man
is dishonorable,

the end of this pig
will go unmourned.

End of the day:
give yourself to your lover

and your leftovers
to the lady upstairs.

Indian Style

Finally, back again to youth, where sneaks
the curious lights of huge doorways
and the clinched plastic comfort
of Velcro collars.

*

Massachusetts has enough trees
for any reasonable man,
enough water to swim in,
enough concrete to hold my feet.

*

With the strength of one thousand turkeys
on a pre-colonial Manhattan Island,
I'll flex my tongues and arms.
When I walk in this city I can imagine no buildings.

Nautical Selection

Standing with his back to the harbor, he addressed
the audience on his times at sea.

His inherited white face, its markings
impressed with the canals and melanoma
of decades of nautical selection,

highball mouthing that indulgence
implicit in mortal correspondence,
his back turned to the coast, then

the harbor lights dimmed.

But looking at the mainland as he was,
to him it was a trick that the eye played on the mind.
"I am old," he thought, "My sight is going."

It was a gift to his audience, it confused him,
they knew; the harbor lights
spread indulgences across their faces.

The harbor lights dimmed,

and for a moment, the sea
was another body, the shore
was another land, and the boats
on the water were other animals.

To own a boat must be a pleasure.

Acknowledgments

Grateful acknowledgment to the editors of the following journals where many of these poems first appeared:

The Naked Ape, Octopus Magazine, Ducky Magazine, Unpleasant Event Schedule, La Petite Zine, Painted Bride Quarterly, Can We Have Our Ball Back?, Kulture Vulture, LIT Magazine, Puppy Flowers, Shampoo Poetry, the tiny, The Good Luck & All the Best, Surgery of Modern Warfare, GoodFoot, No Tell Motel and *The Bedside Guide to No Tell Motel - 2nd Floor.*

Thanks also to those who worked closely with me on these and other poems:

John Cotter, Shanna Compton, Daniel Nester, Jennifer Knox, Marion Wrenn, Maureen Thorson, Erica Kaufman, Mike Sammons, Alexa Vachon, Ada Limon, Austin Kurowski, James Strickland, Andrew Wright, Robert Pham, Gary Petty, Nicholas MacLaren, Gina Myers, Dustin Williamson, Lee Klein, Paul Killebrew, Sam Amadon, Rachael Rakes, Jim Behrle, Brendan Lorber, Tracey McTague, Gabrielle Torres, Sean Welsh, George Murray, Alex Battles, Jamison Driskill, Dan Morrow, Donna Kozloskie, Kevin Caron, Colin Hodges, Joe Hankins, Robert Parent, Derek Mix, Matthew Rohrer and Eddie Berrigan.

Thanks to Reb Livingston, my publisher.

And many thanks and all my love to my incredible family in Texas.

About the Author

Shafer Hall is from Texas. He is a bartender at the Four-Faced Liar
in New York City, where he occasionally curates the Frequency Reading Series. He is a senior editor of *Painted Bride Quarterly*. His poems have appeared in many journals.

photos by Alexa Vachon

Also by No Tell Books

2007

The Bedside Guide to No Tell Motel - 2nd Floor, editors Reb Livingston & Molly Arden

Shy Green Fields, by Hugh Behm-Steinberg

Harlot, by Jill Alexander Essbaum

Blue & Red Roses: Personations, by Karl Parker

The Myth of the Simple Machines, by Laurel Snyder

2006

The Bedside Guide to No Tell Motel, editors Reb Livingston & Molly Arden

Elapsing Speedway Organism, by Bruce Covey

The Attention Lesson, by PF Potvin

Navigate, Amelia Earhart's Letters Home, by Rebecca Loudon

Wanton Textiles, by Reb Livingston & Ravi Shankar

notellbooks.org

Made in the USA
Middletown, DE
19 October 2022

13098228R00052